The Edinburgh
FESTIVAL

The Edinburgh
FESTIVAL

COLOUR MOVES. The world premiere of Robert North's ballet was presented by the Ballet Rambert at the King's Theatre.

A Pictorial Celebration by ROBBIE JACK
words by Owen Dudley Edwards

First published in Great Britain in 1990 by
Canongate Publishing Limited, Edinburgh

Colour illustrations   © Robbie Jack 1990
Introduction   © Owen Dudley Edwards 1990

British Library Cataloguing in Publication Data
Edwards, Owen Dudley
The Edinburgh Festival: a celebration
1. Edinburgh performing arts festivals.
Edinburgh International Festival
I. Title II. Jack, Robbie
791.094134
ISBN 0-86241-327-3

Colour origination by Gorenski Tisk,
Yugoslavia

Half tone origination by Creative Colour,
Glasgow

Printed and bound by Gorenski Tisk,
Yugoslavia

Right: Spirit of the Fringe.

Previous page: A sea of masks provides a dramatic approach to TURANDOT as performed by the Folk Opera of Stockholm at Leith Theatre.

Frank Dunlop, Festival Director, introducing his programme for 1987.

FOREWORD

It is a pleasure and a privilege for me to salute this book. The Edinburgh Festival seems to those of us involved in it as one of the great events in the world's calendar, partly because so many of the world's best creators are celebrated and commemorated in its themes, exhibitions, productions, concerts or coups-de-théatre, partly because it brings together the creators, interpreters and audiences from the whole world in constructive harmony.

The Festival each year revives the richest traditions of the past, makes some of the most provocative cultural assertions of the present and seeks to set in motion chains of ideas and enquiries which will inspire the future.

Everyone's Edinburgh Festival is a different one, both visually and audibly. This book shows, from time to time, in random flashes rather than in any continuous narrative, a view of the Festival through the eyes of a most talented independent observer, the photographer Robbie Jack. His visual record of the Festival is delightfully different from the official or media versions.

The publishers of this book have also drawn extensively on our archives, in the process reprinting some splendid pre-servations of the Festival's triumphs and heroes, above all by two outstanding Festival official photographers, the late Paul Shillabeer, and the very happily living 'Tug' Wilson.

As for our introducer, how can I introduce him? An Irishman with a Welsh name teaching American History at Edinburgh University . . . It sounds like the sort of joke that Festival luminaries as diverse as Samuel Beckett and Ricky Fulton revel in.

It is a great honour for the Festival that Robbie Jack and Canongate have created this record. It is a joy to see through other eyes the wonders of the Festival, and wallow again in those excitements and inspirations. A book, unlike the Festival itself, is there to be dipped into, read, and looked at whenever the reader wishes. The Festivals of the past can live again through books like this.

Frank Dunlop, Director, Edinburgh International Festival.

ACKNOWLEDGEMENTS

Our grateful thanks are due to the Edinburgh Festival Society, to Festival Director Frank Dunlop, CBE, and to his secretary, Linda Crease, to Clive Sandground, Public Relations Consultant to the Festival, and very particularly to Ann Monfries of the Festival Publicity Office, for consistent encouragement in this book's creation, for most generous permission for the use of Festival archives and for specific permission for the reproduction of all pictures other than those by Robbie Jack, for excellent advice and for invaluable answers to many questions. None of them bears responsibility for any opinions, errors, judgements, prognostications or speculations which appear in the introduction or captions. Specific thanks must also go to Mr Dunlop for his foreword, but once again it must be stressed that his kindness in contributing it is not to be misconstrued as an implication that this work of independent observation, verbal and visual, carries the status of an official Festival publication.

The National Library of Scotland has, as ever, been endless in patience and good nature in facilitating research, and in enabling us to draw on its wealth of Festival archive material we became most deeply indebted to Stanley Simpson, of the Department of Manuscripts, whose profound knowledge, boundless generosity and personal kindness made our work so rewarding.

The Edinburgh Room of the Edinburgh Central Library was most helpful and productive in the provision of relevant archival material for the Festival, and for the city.

Mhairi Mackenzie Robinson of the Fringe gave us precious time, while proof reading this year's Fringe programme, to help with the identification of Fringe groups.

It is an honour to include some of the painstaking photographic record of the Festival's early years built up by the late Paul Shillabeer, and we must thank his widow, Mary Shillabeer, for her support and encouragement. It is likewise an honour to reproduce some of the work of the Festival's official photographer of recent years, Alex 'Tug' Wilson, whose infectious good spirits must surely charm his most austere photographic subjects into geniality.

Canongate Publishing would like to thank Mainstream Publishing for their ·warm collegial support´ in permitting Owen Dudley Edwards, under contract to Mainstream for another book on the Festival, to write his introduction and give such further assistance in this book as he was capable of giving. Canongate would also like to thank Bonnie Dudley Edwards, to whom Owen Dudley Edwards is under more permanent contract: so very emphatically would he. His thanks are also due to Allen Wright, prince of Arts Editors, and Roger Savage, incomparable Muse.

Canongate Publishing, Robbie Jack and Owen Dudley Edwards would all like to thank each other, and to assure each other that however irritating they may have been to one another from time to time, it was worth it. They – we – would all, without qualification whatsoever, wish to thank the splendid researcher for this book, Fiona Morrison, who was an endless fountain of ideas, a dauntless enthusiast for the most exhausting quests, and a superb strategist and tactician in every aspect of the book's production.

INTRODUCTION

Reputedly the finest clown in the world,
Oleg Popov, with the Moscow State Circus at the
Playhouse Theatre.

'For three weeks each August, when it holds the most exciting arts
festival in the world, Edinburgh is simply the greatest place on earth.'
Washington Post 1987

*Robert Ponsonby in his last
year as Festival Director.
1960*
PAUL SHILLABEER

*The Earl of Harewood, with
Benjamin Britten, whom
he brought to the Festival
in 1961.*
EIF

Peter Diamand
ROGER PERRY

FESTIVAL DIRECTORS

1947 - 1949	RUDOLF FRANZ JOSEF BING	(born 1902)
1950 - 1955	IAN BRUCE HOPE HUNTER	(born 1919)
1956 - 1960	ROBERT NOEL PONSONBY	(born 1926)
1961 - 1965	GEORGE HENRY HUBERT LASCELLES 7TH EARL OF HAREWOOD	(born 1923)
1966 - 1978	PETER DIAMAND	(born 1913)
1979 - 1983	JOHN RICHARD GRAY DRUMMOND	(born 1934)
1984 -	FRANK DUNLOP	(born 1927)

John Drummond finds a city. EIF

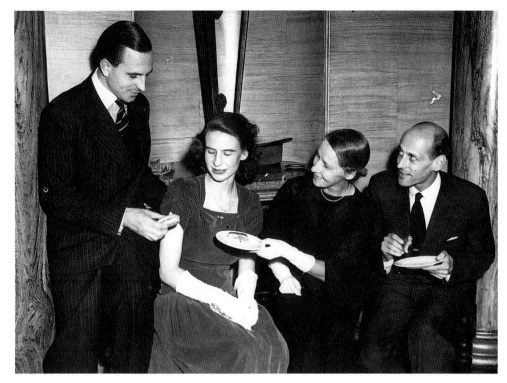

Ian Hunter, Diana Falconer, Nina Bing and Rudolf Bing, pictured at Bing's final Festival. 1949
PAUL SHILLABEER

Rudolf Bing, as founder-director of the Edinburgh Festival and involved in its early plans and dreams from 1944, cast a very long shadow. Like Washington, Bing cannot be compared to his successors save in minor detail: even more important than being the first, his laying of the foundations was what ensured he would not also be the last. His assistant director, Ian Hunter, was the obvious choice to follow him when Bing departed for the Metropolitan Opera in New York although for his first year Hunter was officially 'Artistic Administrator' as was his successor Robert Ponsonby. Hunter, in career terms, was even younger than he looked, war service (whence he emerged a Colonel) having taken years out of his life. Hunter in *Who's Who* includes 'Glyndebourne' among his places of education, and Ponsonby, before he became Director, had spent five years on the Glyndebourne Opera staff as Hunter's assistant. Bing, of course, had been General Manager of Glyndebourne from 1935, a post he held conjointly with Directorship of the Edinburgh Festival. Thus the Glyndebourne connection and, indirectly Bing's influence, lasted for the first decade, and beyond.

Necessarily, Rudolf Bing had had to work his way with the formidable group of Edinburgh dignitaries and intellectuals who had been its co-founders: each learned from the other, and the act of creation had been their joint work. Hunter and Ponsonby were psychologically in more subordinate positions, and yet their Edinburgh overseers were themselves no longer the shapers of the Festival. Its contours had been formed in the Bing years; the 1950s were an affirmation, consolidation and obvious extension of the existing pattern. Ironically, one of the most famous new departures of these years, the 1960 late-night revue *Beyond the Fringe* (with Alan Bennett, Peter Cook, Jonathan Miller and Dudley Moore) showed that Ponsonby's assistant, John Bassett, who commissioned it, might have created other interesting work if appointed Director in natural succession; but by the time *Beyond the Fringe* made headlines the Edinburgh Festival Society had already decided to go for Grand Opera and the Earl of Harewood entered into office fresh from the staff of the Royal Opera House, Covent Garden. At this stage the Director became much more of a personality, all the more so as grandson of King George V. With Harewood, and still more with the austere internationalist Peter Diamand (who was General Manager of the Holland Festival on his appointment), the Director was seen as the Festival's ruler, as the official Festival publications indicated

with 'Director' now heading the page instead of lying at its centre below the Members of Council. The international prestige of the Festival in Diamand's time owed a good deal of the liking it aroused in the international press to the outstanding public relations talents of an Edinburgh journalist, Iain Crawford, his bonhomie and skilful staff organization. He somehow managed to make Diamand sound, if not like an Edinburgh human being, at least like an Edinburgh national monument, difficult, windswept, but immensely prestigious.

The first phase was Bing's long shadow to 1960, the second was the hegemony of Grand Opera to 1978, and the third would be Revolution and Populism under John Drummond and Frank Dunlop. Much of the success of the Edinburgh Festival within and outwith the city depended on many figures other than Directors. Of these the most notable in recent years has been Sheila Colvin, who had once been General Manager of the Traverse Theatre and who rose in a succesion of administrative posts under Drummond and Dunlop until she recently became Director of the Aldeburgh Festival. Her administrative ability and exceptional gifts of diplomacy did much under Drummond and Dunlop to win interest and affection once more in the locality. The enthusiasm with which so many people reacted to the changes made by these two directors was thanks in good part to Sheila

Colvin and both made it clear how much their success must be considered in conjunction with her name.

So what is to be made of the reality behind the Festival's foundation under Bing? The story is complex, the fair dispersal of credit in frequent question, and the relative parts played by quite a large number of people evidently essential. But if any one person is to be called the Father of the Edinburgh Festival it would seem to be Henry Harvey Wood. It begins with Rudolf Bing certainly, brilliant, innovative, impish, Viennese, charming and desperate to find a means of Glyndebourne Opera finding a Festival in which to use its talents; and it was wholly characteristic of him that with the dearth of festivals in war-ravaged Europe and the evident dangers of austerity to the Arts in post-war Britain his answer was to invent one himself. But where? Glyndebourne, like so much else in Britain in 1945, was dominated by a public figure, in this case its owner, John Christie, and it was characteristic of the times that public bodies were similarly identified with specific individuals, the Arts Council, no less, with the name of the great economist Lord Keynes, with whom Christie was at feud. So, in chaos the chimerical reigns; a solution must be sought, if possible, within Britain but beyond Keynes, and perhaps Bing's own birth in the dual monarchy of the Austro-Hungarian Empire naturally led his thoughts to some sort of Budapest, if the equivalent of the Viennese influence made his new Austria an area to be avoided. He looked, too, for an influential Magyar: he got Harvey Wood.

With the circumvention of the Arts Council ('all but adamant against giving money to anything associated with Glyndebourne', stated Bing in his memoirs *5000 Nights at the Opera* [1972]) the British Council seemed the logical place. Harvey Wood, Scottish representative on the British Council, was a figure of remarkable intellectual quality, who had produced a three-volume edition of the works of the English Jacobean playwright John Marston, and was a passionate, quizzical and inspirational enthusiast for Scottish literature. Most important of all, perhaps, in the circumstances, he had exactly the balance of Edinburgh patriotism and administrative realism which the situation needed. The accepted story implies a meeting of minds between Bing and the Lord Provost, John Falconer. The minds met all right, but only when Harvey Wood had found, prepared and cleared a meeting place. Bing thought that St Giles' Cathedral (High Kirk of Edinburgh) was a Roman Catholic institution where the Festival might begin with High Mass while Falconer had never heard of Glyndebourne but had some vague notion that there might have been a festival at Salzburg. (When the Festival was first publicly mooted the local press hung on to Salzburg like a drowning journalist: as the *Glasgow Herald* of November 24th, 1945 put it, with a subtlety Henry James might have envied, 'Edinburgh, it is true, cannot claim, like Salzburg, to be the birthplace of a Mozart; but as a consolation it is worth remembering that the young genius was only too anxious to leave the provincial dullness of his native city behind him.')

Before the Lord Provost could be brought in, Harvey Wood gathered together potential supporters. His own intellectual connections were impeccable: his brother-in-law, for instance, was the deputy librarian and, later, Librarian of the National Library of Scotland. He recruited James Bridie, the playwright; Professor Sidney Newman, Reid Professor of Music at the University of Edinburgh; James Murray Watson, Editor of *The Scotsman* and

much interested in the furtherance of international press co-operation; Mrs Alexander Maitland (whose husband, afterwards knighted, was soon to become Deputy Chairman of the Royal Bank of Scotland); the Countess of Rosebery, daughter-in-law of a former Prime Minister and herself an intimate of Queen Elizabeth, Consort of King George VI; Stewart Deas, the Literary Editor of *The Scotsman* (and soon to become Professor of Music at Sheffield); Sheriff John Cameron, afterwards the great Scottish judge, Lord Cameron, who would play so significant a part in the investigation of conditions in Northern Ireland; and behind them he had others on whose goodwill he might draw, including Sir John Fraser, the Principal of Edinburgh University, its Professors of English and French Literature, the head of the Royal Scottish Academy, and the Curator of the National Gallery of Scotland. Falconer was a magnificent voice for their combined talents and he knew how to talk the language of invisible assets in tourism, prestige, patriotism, civic spirit, and even world leadership.

They were all of them desperately conscious of the possible place of Edinburgh as a lighthouse of cultural survival in a world

Bruno Walter, reunited with the Vienna Philharmonic Orchestra from which he had been driven by Nazi persecution, launched the first Festival with Gustav Mahler's DAS LIED VON DER ERDE. 1949
EIF

THE COCKTAIL PARTY by T.S. Eliot was the first play to receive a premiere performance at the Edinburgh Festival, which it did under the direction of E. Martin Browne with settings by Anthony Holland, produced by Henry Sherek. The cast of THE COCKTAIL PARTY, here shown in performance at the 1949 Festival, included Robert Flemyng, Cathleen Nesbitt, Irene Worth, Ernest Clark, Donald Houston and Christina Horniman.
PAUL SHILLABEER

Tyrone Guthrie who adapted THE THRIE ESTAITES for its first modern revival in 1948 at the Hall of the General Assembly of the Church of Scotland .
PAUL SHILLABEER

Glyndebourne Opera firmly maintained the place in the Festival for which Bing had conjured the Festival up and in 1953 it performed, among other offerings, Stravinsky's THE RAKE'S PROGRESS with Auden's libretto. Carl Ebert conducted and the designers included Osbert Lancaster.
EIF

where but a few short months before every human decency seemed on the verge of extinction. There was something of an assumption that Munich's, Bayreuth's, Salzburg's losses would be Edinburgh's gain: but even stronger was the sense of their own place in Europe and the obligation on them to bring healing because they had been spared. Bing from the first made much of this, and his own Viennese identity he frankly placed in the forefront of his negotiations. Hitler's foul legislation and persecution against the Jews had driven the great Bruno Walter from his own Vienna Philharmonic Orchestra: he, Bing, would bring them together again, and would do it here, in Edinburgh. Falconer, who had never heard of Bruno Walter, was beside himself with gratification: the name meant nothing, but he understood the thing, and that was what mattered.

Bing was to have the Festival organized under the Glyndebourne administration (which, after all, was Bing), but he played the Lord Provost, the unofficial advisers (now formed into the Edinburgh Festival Society)

and the City Council, with a dexterity which might have moved the admiration of Talleyrand. He drew up plans and costed them to the satisfaction of the City Treasurer– without including opera. He would go ahead on all fronts, captivating them with possible beguiling alternatives, discussing the case for this against that, apologising most prettily when he once again called them English, but always holding opera back – no doubt with explanations of its exorbitant cost. As a result, they did not merely ask for Glyndebourne Opera, they demanded it. Were they quite sure? Bing almost turned devil's advocate. It was the last straw. The last straw would cost £10,000, Bing was careful to point out. And what could be more appropriate than Glyndebourne's *La Nozze di Figaro*, by their own non-native son Mozart, unless it be Verdi's *Macbeth*? Bing had at last found a meaning for Scotland in his normal range of interests.

It took from November 1945 to August 1947 to create the first Festival and as one looks over the list of that year's offerings well does it seem the organisers were justified in

their Songs of Praise which opened it in St Giles' Cathedral (presumably without simultaneous Latin for Bing's benefit). The very sense of the wound in the war-torn Earth forcing its lacerated edges together characterises the makers, the city, the artists, the press, the public: artists came to affirm that the wound had to close, none more symbolically than in the glorious, rich voice of Kathleen Ferrier singing Gustav Mahler's *Das Lied von der Erde* : Walter's reunion with the Vienna Philharmonic should not, after all, be purely nostalgic but should have a voice of the future – only six more years of the future for poor Kathleen Ferrier, as it would prove – but a Festival starting its life on that voice could never ask for greater however long it may live.

Queen Elizabeth was duly present, and became Patron, another symbol of recovery from war. She had interpreted her duty from start to finish to stand by her people, stating during the war 'the children will stay with me, and I will stay with the King'. It was in the same spirit that she came to Edinburgh's attempt to bind up the wounds of war and make beauty grow from them. Undoubtedly her support was a vital consideration in making the Festival generally accepted as a sacrament of recovery and reconciliation.

Monarchy is normally kept away from anything without certain assurance of popularity and success. Elizabeth, the Queen Consort, backed the Festival at the planning stage when success was anything but certain: her support played its part in creating the bandwagon which made success. And following her leadership other Royal figures made their appearance: her daughter, Princess Margaret, her sister-in-law, the Princess Royal, and the Princess Royal's son, George, Earl of Harewood not long released from being a Nazi prisoner-of-war.

This was, socially speaking, on the highest level: but there had been incessant activity on innumerable other levels. They brought Todd Duncan, the American black singer of Negro spirituals, thus making it a truly international Festival, declared Bing in putting Duncan's name before the committee. They accepted a request from the Glasgow Orpheus Choir that it make an appearance and, after some dubious backing and filling, they mounted a concert of Scots Gaelic songs. They decided on having exhibitions in which, as the Curator of the National Gallery told them, 'the representation of certain artists in the collection would be augmented'. They encouraged what they called 'subsidiary events', working like demons to bring the

them *The Queen's Comedy* performed by his Citizens' Theatre Company of Glasgow the year before he died. They went for a couple of Shakespeares, taking account of considerable popular demand, to be performed by the Old Vic Company: Ralph Richardson's production of *Richard II* and *The Taming of the Shrew*. They had some hopes of Gielgud's new company but these faded. Alfred Lunt and Lynn Fontanne agreed to bring a play, but it turned out this would be Terence Rattigan's *Love in Idleness* (or *O Mistress Mine*) whose famous erotic scene on stage played by the two leads was only partly respectabilized by their real-life marriage. The sub-committee (consisting at that point of Bridie, Newman and the head of the Royal Scottish Academy) declined the play and, therefore, the Lunts, despite Bing's protests. They ended up with Louis Jouvet's company from Paris playing Moliere's *Ecole des Femmes* (thus remotely influencing many subsequent, successful versions of it in Scots), and Giradoux's *Ondine* for which they needed the intervention of the French Ambassador.

The whole thing, in retrospect, sounds like a cross between the First Crusade and the Stroganoff Ballet. A few years later the Festival Society was nominated for the Nobel Peace Prize by Scotland's winner of the Prize in 1949, Lord Boyd Orr. It seems like a monumental piece of cheek; it also seems hauntingly appropriate. Yet in a sense it was not the Society, although this was a very

Edinburgh studies the Renoir Exhibition in 1953.
PAUL SHILLABEER

The exhibition of mediaeval Yugoslav frescoes was an extraordinary revelation of international transportation of masterpieces as seen by this fragment of a Pieta. 1953
PAUL SHILLABEER

Marcel Marceau, presented LES PANTOMIMES DE BIP, a welcome visitor in 1953 and 1948.
EIF

number up to fifty (which led to the inclusion of the National Library of Scotland under this heading), wholly unaware that thereby they were producing the first pre-natal manifesto of the future Largest Show on Earth, the Edinburgh Festival Fringe (destined to surface in 1948). They besought the Chamber of Commerce to induce local shopkeepers to mount 'window displays of a dignified nature' during the Festival period (a proceeding they discussed under the general heading of exhibitions). They arranged for the opening of private squares and, even, of private art collections in private houses. They argued about the theatre.

Bridie had hoped to write them a play but that had to wait until 1950 when he gave

The Sadler's Wells Ballet, an old friend of the Festival, returned yet again, under the direction of Ninette de Valois, with LE LAC DES CYGNES starring Margot Fonteyn. 1956
PAUL SHILLABEER

The Festival broke the parochialism of restriction to Europe when the Ram Gopal Indian Ballet performed THE LEGEND OF TAJ MAHAL, created by Ram Gopal himself. 1956
PAUL SHILLABEER

hardworking institution in the process of creation, but the city itself which had made the Festival happen. Edinburgh was too cranky to build anything like the needful venues in subsequent years (the long protracted dispute about an Opera House is famous simply because of opera's customary commandeering of publicity: what was actually under discussion was a massive Festival Centre which would also have involved a theatre and, to this day, Edinburgh has nothing to touch the Dundee Repertory Theatre in beauty, acoustics, immediacy and imagination). It was, as Sir Thomas Beecham said, madness to expect Edinburgh to host a Festival when it was too mean to take fundamental action for decent venues. Yet the impossible continued to happen, while the obvious was ignored. Judging by some of the designs for the Festival Centre which have survived and the sight of what the city and the University perpetrated in the name of architecture during the 1950s and 1960s, we may have more cause to be grateful for what did not happen than we know. It annoyed Festival-goers like Mr Bernard Levin who passionately denounced Edinburgh for its vandalism and parsimony while being unable to remember which end of the town he was talking about.

But in bringing the Festival to birth Harvey Wood, Bing and their colleagues had actually shown how the city could come into creative life. It is important to stress that at this point the warring institutions do seem to have operated together, not so much as boards as through individuals who could move their own circles. The music professor, the banker's wife, the Queen's friend, the doctor playwright, the newspaper editor, the Lord Provost, the scholar in the British Council, the opera manager in search of an outlet – among them they made a city make a Festival – a Festival of Music, anyway. It had a little way to go to be a true Festival of Drama. The following year Bing would bring in Tyrone Guthrie who would recruit the assistance of the playwright Robert Kemp (ultimately Bridie's replacement as drama adviser), to adapt for the modern stage Sir David Lyndsay's *Ane Satyre of the Thrie Estaites*. And in Bing's last year, 1949, festival drama obtained one of its greatest coups: the premiere of T. S. Eliot's The Cocktail Party directed by E. Martin Browne. In 1953 Browne's direction of *The Confidential Clerk* was also a Festival premiere.

Sir John Falconer retired from office in 1947 (and died in 1954) although his successors continued to follow in his

enthusiastic footsteps. Harvey Wood after continued resourceful chairmanship of the programme committee was transferred to Paris in 1950. Bridie died in 1951. Fraser's successors at the University showed little interest, and the huge academic intake of the next decades, proving largely English in composition, tended to migrate south during the long vacation. The University lost its involvement with the Festival, as it lost its identification with the city. Murray Watson died in harness at *The Scotsman* in 1955; Deas had gone to Sheffield in 1949. *The Scotsman* would retain its interest, but more as a critic than as a creator, although its music critic continued to supervise the programme layout throughout the Diamand years. The creative work of *The Scotsman* , in fact, turned more to the Fringe and, under the Arts Editorship of Allen Wright it played a vital part in the establishment of a nucleus of critical standards for the Fringe, that extraordinary phenomenon, and in the encouragement of original work on it, but that is another story. Professor Newman, Lady Rosebery, and Lord Cameron remained, among Harvey Wood's happy band, but their role became increasingly one of endorsement. The Festival became a great international event.

And then, in 1979, it changed.

The transformation of the Festival in the 1980s turned on many points but the central one was its sense of Scottishness. It had been expressed before, intermittently, but 1979 was the key year, Festival Director John Drummond's first, and from his tumultuous entry on his charge it became in its entirety a Festival of life. Scotland's greatest poet of the twentieth century, Hugh MacDiarmid, having frequently lambasted the Festival as a Laputa, a flying island touching down virtually without recognition of where it was, died during the 1978 Festival. One year later, his widow Valda Grieve, speaking after a Festival celebration of her husband's work in St Cecilia's Hall, said that had he lived to see John Drummond in action he would have hailed him as the bringer of the Festival Scotland needed.

John Drummond, half Scots, half Australian, product of Cambridge, Paris and London, saw himself more as the disciple of Diaghilev than Yeats, but he had Yeats's, and MacDiarmid's, conviction of strength-

ening national culture by cosmopolitanism, and Yeats's readiness to pursue fascinating counterparts in indigenous cultural self-realisation to all corners of the globe. MacDiarmid proclaimed an affinity between Scotland and Georgia; coincidentally, Drummond's first year brought the Rustaveli Theatre of Georgia to play Shakespeare's *Richard III* (and Brecht's *The Caucasian Chalk Circle*) to Edinburgh audiences. The Georgians bellowed their identities at one another at an early moment. After that, it was up to the audience to trust their comprehension to faith, like novices floating on calm water, and watch the fascinating mixture of familiar and unfamiliar action bring Shakespeare alive in an utterly alien language. It was an extraordinary success, once the fear of the unknown had been silenced by ecstatic notices and the half-empty auditorium of the first nights gave way to packed houses by the end.

'Trust me!' said Drummond afterwards, in his pursuit of the remotest cultures, and we trusted him. His judgement could always be depended on in foreign-language theatre, provided he had seen it himself: the only real production disasters of his time were when he had not, and his apparently boundless energy and suspected ambition to be in Vancouver and Bucharest at the same time meant that, where possible, he went, he saw, he brought. And he fought for outstanding Scottish material, always hunting for originality, not always succeeding in his efforts to induce its birth and Festival epiphany, loudly denouncing parochialism in Edinburgh, London, Paris, New York or any other lairs, always loving Scotland and wounded by it as only one who loves it can be wounded.

In music he broke the Bach-to-Bartok barrier, which had cocooned the Festival in recent years, and voyaged into ancient and modern territory so long closed to Festival music-lovers. He took opera from its gluttonous eminence in which it had gorged itself at the rest of the Festival's expense, and went for work of ideas and acting strength where, formerly, the charmed circle had gibbered of tenors and sopranos in language more calculated to repel than to make converts. Kent Opera might seem a poor substitute for La Scala but it was truly something to see in Jill Gomez a Traviata who really seemed a tuberculosis victim instead of the usual duel between orchestra and bedsprings in counter-assertions of the prima donna's demise.

Drummond's greatest year was his last, 1983, when his theme of 'Vienna 1900' virtually made one great city in its cultural pre-eminence settle down on another (it was a highly symbolic final theme from the Festival's redeemer since its creator, Bing, was born in Vienna in 1902). Opera, theatre, lectures, discussions, swirled in solar system around a gigantic exhibition which seemed to reveal the Director as adding the arts of Attila and Sobieski to his normal embodiment of Yeats, MacDiarmid, Diaghilev and Napoleon: the entire Schoenbrun palace appeared to have been carried to Edinburgh on his ample shoulders. As his own performances in lectures, seminars and press conferences testified, Drummond was above all else a magnificent teacher, and one whose inspiration made the Festival's vibrations radiate in influence far beyond the Fringe (whose work he enthusiastically championed and whose influence he strongly acknowledged), to surface in festival locations elsewhere in Scotland, Britain and across the globe. Glasgow's Mayfest, Garden Festival, and even City of Culture status owe much to Glasgow civic pride from which complacent Edinburgh has all too much to learn: but they also owe far more than Glasgow or Edinburgh realise to the currents, the search for originality, the sheer vitality, of John Drummond.

It was one hell of an act to follow; but that cliché misleads by prompting comparisons which evolution makes into nonsense. Frank Dunlop, arriving in 1984, differed outwardly more than inwardly from John Drummond: in philosophy they were very close. And Dunlop continued much of what Drummond started, fighting as Drummond had fought to make Festival culture a live and challenging business instead of an attractive museum of proven and far-acclaimed success. Dunlop's own production of Weber's *Oberon*, for instance, carried on the work of constructive iconoclasm. The Usher Hall, long hallowed in its reverential and relentless respectability, to unhallowed eyes more concerned with the evening shirts of the performers than with their performance, now confronted an opera thrown on its majestic concert stage, and the brilliant and diminutive Seiji Ozawa conducting, not only his Boston Symphony Orchestra, but also the very actors and singers whose elaborate mythological demands hurtled them around the musicians.

Dunlop pursued Drummond's quest for new theatre space, and with greater success. Drummond had done great things with the Moray House Gymnasium, notably in housing the Edinburgh Traverse Theatre production of Tom McGrath's *Animal*, a play about apes

H. R. H. Prince Philip, Duke of Edinburgh, and husband of the present Queen congratulating Clive Morton. 1960
PAUL SHILLABEER

The world premiere of Sydney Goodsir Smith's THE WALLACE, A Triumph in Five Acts, commissioned for the 1960 Festival, with Iain Cuthbertson in the title role seen here awaiting sentence from Clive Morton as Edward I, who takes counsel before ordering the symbol of Scottish nationalism to be hanged, castrated and disembowelled.
PAUL SHILLABEER

Not Brecht, not Beckett, not even Boucicault, but La Compagnie Roger Planchon in Dumas's LES TROIS MOUSQUETAIRES adapted by Roger Planchon and starring Roger Planchon with Jean-Jacques Lagarde, Armand Meffre, and Jean Baptiste Thierree, all three in the title role - all for one, one for all - directed by Roger Planchon. 1960
EIF

(breaking an even more formidable language frontier) whose achievement had so drastically (if in performance so successfully) depended on intricate movement worked out by Stuart Hopps and precision-timed direction from Chris Parr. But Dunlop went much further afield in discovering St Bride's, a hall from which even the hardiest spirits of the Fringe had shuddered away, and inaugurated it with the Krakow Theatre's Polish-language version of Dostoevsky's *Crime and Punishment* in which the audience was made to sit on hard long forms and suffer some of the rigours of juries reminiscent of the days when wretches hanged that jurymen might dine. The customers joyfully, if somewhat arthritically, testified to the force and terrifying immediacy with which the book's purpose had been realised. Dunlop kept St Bride's and cultivated creature comforts: racked seating

on chairs with the luxury of backs allowed a more Castilian contemplation of Calderon's curiously reverential ideas about Henry VIII in *Schism in England* translated by Edinburgh playwright John Clifford; more predictably Calderon, as well as Clifford and Linda Bassett, realised the nobility of Henry's Spanish Catherine. The Leith Theatre, too, pressed into Dunlop's service, strengthened the revival of the port so long oppressed by the jealous capital which ultimately engulfed it. There Dunlop fulfilled a dream Drummond had long cherished without success by bringing a Chinese theatre company with its extraordinary interpretation of *Macbeth*.

Dunlop, indeed, could claim to have smashed the hoodoo on *Macbeth*, so long timorously unspoken in name by actors in recognition of the mysterious (and not so mysterious) disasters associated with its productions, and to have done so in Scotland's, if not Macbeth's, capital. The Toho Theatre Company of Japan made several visits to Edinburgh during his regime. The great courtyard of Edinburgh University's Old College became a theatre, and Drummond's quiet luring back of University interest from apparent indifference into Festival concern now found fruit in Dunlop's outstanding realisation of the production possibilities of the University's power centre. An enthusiastic lover of the Festival in the University Secretary, Alex Currie, and an endlessly resourceful University Information officer, Ray Footman, were leaders among those making possible Toho's *Medea* whose culmination in the rescue of Medea by her fiery dragon at last brought into full expression the intentions of Euripides formulated over two thousand years earlier. It was proof that by becoming itself more conscious of Scotland the Festival was inducing increasing Scottishness in Edinburgh's more deScottified institutions. Two years later the Playhouse Theatre housed Toho's successor company's *The Tempest*, whose opening in a further triumph of Japanese theatre technology gave a tempest in two minutes to strike awe into the most cynical heart. But the Toho *Macbeth* paved the way for all that followed that time in the Lyceum which had given of its plenty to the roll of previous disastrous productions. The bloody child, horrifyingly, was an enormous foetus, and the entire production keenly sympathetic to Japanese Samurai traditions. The audience hung on every bloodstained word. For the first time, in all probability, an audience heard the owl scream and the cricket cry at the moment of Duncan's murder, and so well were emotions telegraphed that one could assert the exact moment when Macduff's suspicions of Macbeth were first silently aroused. Press personnel were further disconcerted when Mikijiro Hira, the toweringly dominating Macbeth (who would later play Medea) proved in private a gentle and self-deprecating figure, as indeed had been Ramas Chkikvadze, the Rustaveli Richard, Czar-like on stage, unobtrusive off.

Frank Dunlop, Scottish on his father's side like Drummond, is a more conspicuously populistic figure. Cambridge at its most exciting in student theatre left the strongest educational mark on Drummond: Dunlop is a much more obviously self-educated person, having learned to read books from the set of Dickens his socialist father received as a subscriber to the old *Daily Herald*. Either

Four more Muskateers: Dudley Moore, Alan Bennett, Peter Cook and Jonathan Miller open their diverse careers as BEYOND THE FRINGE, commissioned for the first week at the Royal Lyceum Theatre in 1960.
EIF

Marlene Dietrich says farewell to Edinburgh in late-night entertainment at the Royal Lyceum Theatre. 1965
PAUL SHILLABEER

man would have been naturally led to co-operation with the University and enthusiasm for its traditions of the late eighteenth-century Scottish Enlightenment. Dunlop became enthralled by the great figures of the Enlightenment and its arguments without end which proved so constructive in cumulative results. He profited by the University celebrations of the Enlightenment in 1986, mounted a splendid example of Enlightenment theatre symbolically staged as a drawing-room entertainment in the appropriate architectural surroundings of the Signet Library with a production of the Reverend John Home's *Douglas* first staged in Edinburgh in 1756 (when, allegedly, it elicited the defiant Scots cry of 'whaur's yer Wullie Shakespeare noo?'). He hosted, too, the Daiches-Jones 'Hotbed of Genius' Exhibition in which the Enlightenment was reborn in the ears of the promenaders in an artifically haunted house, and he brought the explosively inspirational Nicholas Phillipson in a lecture at the Royal Museum of Scotland. The way had been opened for Dunlop through a University struggling to get back

L'ENSEMBLE NATIONAL
DES BALLETS DU SENEGAL
in the Royal Lyceum
Theatre. The Driankes,
young women famous for
their elegance, are
assembled for the Sabar.
1972
PAUL SHILLABEER

Claudia McNeil as Sister
Margaret in the AMEN
CORNER by the American
novelist James Baldwin. As
a polemicist for black rights
and social analyst of race
relations, Baldwin was one
of the most exciting
challenges to his time.
Royal Lyceum Theatre
1965
PAUL SHILLABEER

into its parent city. The great critic David Daiches, the philosopher Peter Jones and his wife, Anne, had asserted the Enlightenment's place in the University's past by a series of seminars and lectures all that year, and the exhibition which brought the old philosophers and scientists within the grasp of ordinary Scots and non-Scots alike was but the culmination.

Similarly the art historian Duncan Macmillan made the most of the University's David Talbot Rice Gallery and magnificently-ceilinged Upper Library Hall with a captivating and profound work of social history in the exhibition of Scottish nineteenth-century painting, where aesthetics opened up to the world so much that arid textbooks had closed, stressing the importance of the Scottish cultural past in its own right. Macmillan could show that a given painting might be no mute, inglorious Leonardo, but it could say so much about what made human beings and their society live and grow.

The Hall of the General Assembly of the Church of Scotland has been hosting Festival productions since 1948. To have brought such a thing to pass at all was a revolution, and like other revolutions in the Church of Scotland, it was primarily the work of a

woman, yet, like most work done by women, the credit for it was subsequently given to men. The idea and the first steps towards its realisation came from Sadie Aitken, Manager of the Gateway Theatre until it closed in 1965, and subsequently Festival Manager of St Cecilia's Hall in the Cowgate (where famous readings took place, including Tom Fleming's great recital of Hugh MacDiarmid's *A Drunk Man Looks at the Thistle* performed before its appreciative author in 1977). Sadie (apologies for use of the first name but her ghost would leave me no peace were I to call her 'Aitken') combined, at will, a towering Edimbourgeoise respectability and a flow of naturalistic expression which could pulverize any actor or journalist. In 1948, Sadie, faced by worried Festival and civic worthies fussing about wherever Tyrone Guthrie could stage the medieval playwright Sir David Lyndsay's *Ane Satyre of the Thrie Estaites*, declared for the Assembly Hall and threw her church-womanship into the manufacture of the necessary channels to bring the Moderator and his advisers into diplomatic negotiation with Lord Provost, producer and Festival Director. Once one considers the matter, her claim to have been the vital agent and the

initial inspiration is impossible to gainsay. Sadie knew that the basis of Scottish Presbyterianism is not to function on decisions handed down from on high but to cherish the sentiments of the laity. She could know, as the great men of the Festival could not know, what the real hopes were for an agreement from the Church authorities and she spoke with a clear, professional, non-political voice representative of conventional Edinburgh. She could think of the Assembly Hall as an insider aware of its possibilities, not as an outsider hoping to make a raid. Once she had opened up the way, Tyrone Guthrie could be relied upon to talk in an appropriately Calvinistic strain which in any case motivated his thought much more powerfully than secular critics have realised. *The Thrie Estaites* could readily be declared a play showing the Scottish people hungering for the Reformation in strongly popular terms; it is in fact a ribald anti-clerical parable devised by a shrewd courtier to show the Scottish Crown the pickings to be obtained from the clergy. The case for its performance, and its constant revival, very notably by Frank Dunlop in Tom Fleming's productions of 1984 and 1985, rests on its supreme dramatic quality, its deployment of a whole variety of characters in a variety of scientific realisations from pageant to psychology, and its rich evolution from the whole medieval tradition of theological personification. And it has some good hard points to make against bureaucratic hypocrisy in any age: it is all too appropriate that Fleming's production subsequently toured with great success in Poland.

Having undone the hostility of her Church to the presentation of God's creatures in creations of their own, Sadie Aitken could look on with satisfaction at subsequent Festivals as the General Assembly extended its permission to cover frankly secular works. She was still alive when Dunlop brought back the play she had worked so effectively to help revive from its four hundred year silence, but her courageous embodiment of the spirit of Edinburgh at its noblest had ended when, a few years later, Dunlop staged his own production of Schiller's *Maria Stuart* with Hannah Gordon as the eponymous, if historically questionable, symbol of Catholicism in the Scottish Reformation.

The production came under fire from its critics, and here the Director's dilemma of

limited time militated against critical success although midway through the Festival the production found its way and audiences subsequently acclaimed it. The magnificent use of Assembly space to polarize Mary confronting her English cousin and subsequent executioner, Elizabeth (in Schiller's ruthless defiance of the historical fact that they never met), radiated electricity enough to light the entire Fringe and Mary's hiss of the name of Elizabeth's mother, Anne Boleyn, had all the force of what Dorothy Parker termed in another context a citation of an adversary's 'canine ancestry on the distaff

Frank Dunlop's Young Vic production BIBLE ONE at Haymarket Ice Rink. 1972
PAUL SHILLABEER

TAMBURLAINE THE GREAT, Christopher Marlowe's play as realised in the Hall of the General Assembly of the Church of Scotland by The Glasgow Citizens' Theatre Company. 1972
PAUL SHILLABEER

side'. The year preceding the four hundredth anniversary of Mary's execution in 1587 had brought Russian opera on the same theme to the King's Theatre. It was a splendid pageant, exceptionally clever in using different levels to enable Mary and Elizabeth to be counterpointed on the stage without ever appearing to be in the same town, while a splendidly Rasputin-like John Knox harangued his Protestant followers who then (recalling the habits of their Russian Orthodox ancestors) devoutly crossed themselves.

How far has the Festival been successful in its use of contemporary Scottish theatre? Writing in 1977, David Hutchison declared morosely in his *The Modern Scottish Theatre* that 'The Edinburgh Festival's contribution to Scottish theatre has been disappointing...The official festival usually presents a Scottish play, but all too often the plays chosen are such that they would never have appeared were there not the necessity to put on Scottish work of some description.' In a work of gallant brevity, Hutchison could not readily exceptionalise: and his bleak summation testifies additionally to the great transformation Drummond inaugurated two years later.

In fact, Dunlop was able to draw on at least one other great achievement of former years in addition to *The Thrie Estaites* – *The*

Wallace – directed by Tom Fleming as his second Assembly Hall offering in 1985. The poet Sydney Goodsir Smith had written it for the Festival in 1960, and the spirit of the most altruistic leader of Scotland's Wars of Independence against Edward I of England harmonised eloquently with the ideas of John-the-Common-Weal employed by Lyndsay and strongly celebrated in their own right in Fleming's *The Thrie Estaites*. MacDiarmid's friend the playwright had died in 1975, and it was left to his widow, the schoolteacher Hazel Goodsir Smith, to salute the new Scottish consciousness in the Festival in the knowledge that her husband, too, would have rejoiced in it. Sydney Goodsir Smith's sense of the complex of emotions battling with patriotism was eloquently realised in the production, from Leonard Maguire's significantly vulnerable Edward I to Roy Hanlon's hold on the tortured logic behind Menteith's betrayal of Wallace. The great revivals had inspirational roles to play in the further development of modern Scottish Nationalism, but their most enduring effect must have been the subtlety of their psychology, all the more remarkable from an actor-director of Fleming's natural force. Boldness of approach was to be expected from him: what was outstanding was his mastery of detail and its cohesion without obliteration in the clear lines of his strategy. In *The Wallace* , in particular, Fleming showed his ability to use the great space of the Assembly Hall to realise a vast moral loneliness in courage.

To readers of the most authoritative recent account of the Festival within hard covers, Lord Harewood's memoirs *The Tongs and the Bones* (1981), the above must seem as though we have been attending different Festivals (as his lordship's successor as Festival Artistic Director, Peter Diamand, used to remark acidly in speaking of press coverage of his own offerings). Some music-lovers with long memories hail Harewood's time as the zenith of musical achievement at the Festival, and it is certainly not his book's fault if they do not. His concerts were adventurous in their attacks on space and time: his use of Indian music and dance, and accompanying exhibition, was an important precedent for Drummond's conquests, although man for man it may be doubted if on his own showing Harewood's evangelical capacities approach Drummond's devastating zeal for mass infection with his enthusiasms Harewood's account is a remarkable recital of success in many different musical spheres but the abiding impression left is that the Festival was *his*, where Drummond habitually

thundered that it was *yours*. Many of the great conductors Harewood brought, such as Carlo Maria Guilini and Pierre Boulez, would return under his friend Diamand, although the range of composition repertoire dwindled in Diamand's long reign. Boulez, in particular, became a great Festival figure, ever-ready to provide exciting discussions of the works he conducted with characteristic batonless exhuberance and force.

If Diamand's subordination of all else to opera divided the multitude from the aficionadi, common ground could be obtained in universal admiration for Claudio Abbado as conductor of *Carmen* even when the voraciously expensive, if magnificent, and would-be naturalistic production starring Teresa Berganza and Placido Domingo (and an almost incredibly Nixon-lookalike Escamillo) was ruthlessly brought back a second year (1977 and 1978): Drummond happily hosted Abbado in subsequent years, minus *Carmen*. Diamand opera could be wonderful – the hearts Berganza captured so bewitchingly as Carmen had only just recovered from their enslslement to her gamin-like Cherubino in *The Marriage of Figaro* alongside the godlike Puckishness of Sir Geraint Evans and the rich cadences of Dietrich Fischer-Dieskau – but its com-

Festival Fringe Chairman, Andrew Cruickshank, the veteran Scottish actor seen in Sir David Lyndsay's THE THRIE ESTAITES, directed by Tom Fleming at the Hall of the General Assembly of the Church of Scotland. 1984
ALEX 'TUG 'WILSON

Placido Domingo as Don Jose and Teresa Berganza as Carmen in Bizet's CARMEN conducted by Claudio Abbado. 1977
ALEX 'TUG' WILSON

Derek Jacobi as Hamlet and an unidentified performer as Yorick in the Prospect Theatre production of HAMLET, Hall of the General Assembly of the Church of Scotland, 1977.
ALEX 'TUG' WILSON

And it's 'banzai' to you too, when Birnam Wood shall come to Dunsinain. The Toho Theatre Company of Japan in MACBETH, a play for once given a chance to delight a Royal Lyceum Theatre audience. 1985
ALEX 'TUG' WILSON

placency probably drove the final nails into the coffin of the long-debated plans for an Edinburgh Opera House. The humiliation of theatre had not begun with Diamand, however, and, in certain respects, his assistant, Bill Thomley, did something to begin that humiliation's end. It was he, indeed, who brought in Frank Dunlop's production of *Joseph and his Amazing Technicolor Dreamcoat*

'Drama, I quickly found out', noted the autobiographical Earl, ' was considered the poor relation in Edinburgh programming.' Elsewhere he mentions that having declared the South Indian Temple dancer Balasarawati ' one of the three greatest living dancers' in his Festival brochure he was asked, ' who said it?', and replied 'I did'. It would seem that this supplies at least one name of those who considered drama the poor relation. His lordship's only allusion to a specific theatre production title is a reference to *Beyond the Fringe* brought to the Festival by his predecessor. He mentions the late night shows at the Lyceum, recalls Juliette Greco, Amelia Rodrigues and (venomously) Marlene Dietrich on whom he revenged himself by 'circulating the rumour that reports about her age were greatly exaggerated, she was in truth only just over fifty' (she was sixty-five at the time). Such courtesies apart, he says nothing of drama beyond remarking that he used three theatres for it: like Gallio, he cared for none of these things. The late-night

shows, by Diamand's penultimate year, had trickled down to Max Wall's embarrassing impressions of Buster Keaton and it was Dunlop who showed what could be done to emancipate theatre celebrities from the obvious by bringing back Wall to triumph in Beckett's *Malone Dies*. Even that was itself overshadowed by the high point of the Beckett material Dunlop unleashed in the same first year of his tenure: the Harold Clurman Theatre of New York in a number of short Beckett plays in which the combination of spot lighting and the immeasurably sensitive inflection of the voice of David Warrilow elicited the miniature delicacy of Beckett's composition. (The more ribald critics enjoyed spreading that year's rumours to the effect that the anchorite playwright was about to make a descent on the Festival, and legend insists that two journalists from the *Daily Express* sat haplessly at Edinburgh Airport for an entire day – Waiting for Beckett.)

The change in the Festival star billing from music and, ultimately, opera to high focus on theatre derived from the mushroom growth of the Fringe which as showcase of drama's future waxed stronger with each deepening furrow of Festival contempt. In the end, Ponsonby's famous revue became all too ironic a comment on Festival theatre: Festival theatre was not beyond the Fringe, it was light-years behind it. 'I had no grudge whatsoever against the Fringe', remarks the

indifferent Harewood, adding significantly 'but when I arrived it was officially very much frowned on'. The frowns continued after his departure, but the indifference could not sustain itself. Diamond, probably to his vast surprise, briefly found himself a hero in the cause of theatrical freedom when the censorious suddenly swung their guns at him, and Ian McKellen's haunting *Edward II* was denounced in terms usually restricted to the Fringe as redolent of more of this filth habitually churned out nowadays from London. The indignant town councillor in question, much valued by Fringe companies for his publicity-winning denunciations, was not greatly disconcerted by the information that Christopher Marlowe, like Lewis Carroll's pig, had been dead for some years: he probably considered it hitting below the belt which, in the circumstances of Edward II's demise as depicted on stage would have been accurate enough. Drummond brought McKellen back for a quite phenomenally realistic performance as D. H. Lawrence but by this time the councillor knew where Marlowe – and Lawrence – had gone.

Drama still had many dismal hours under Diamond – there was a *Tempest* quite as memorable in its way as that Japanese production under Dunlop's aegis but for diametrically opposite reasons. Yet experimentalism from time to time found its way to the official programme. The Ronconi version of *Orlando Furioso* astounded and delighted its audience, although the powerful production machinery of conception proved disastrous when a return visit turned Aristophanean subtlety into Brobdingnagian

ponderousness. A rock musical of the *Pilgrim's Progress* with music by Carl Davis had some remarkable *coups de theatre*. It gave an added dimension to Bunyan's theatre-hating dramatic genius.

But what ailed the Festival theatre in those years was its knowledge of the Festival directorial diagnosis of its absence of general intrinsic interest. Sometimes, great names hit the stage in the strait-jackets fashioned by purblind direction. Scottish material was even more pointedly slung out for its audiences as fare for the hopelessly parochial. The Drummond revolution, when it came, was all the more effective because its maker was a passionate enthusiast for music but one who also believed that the Fringe was the friend and benefactor of the Festival, not its enemy, and that Scotland must be served with work that could stand up to comparison with the theatre of any other country, not simply solaced by some latter-day Kailyard box-office fodder. It was a revolution which knew when to build on its predecessors' accomplishments as well as when to jettison them. It recalled something of Harewood's interest in dance as well as music experimentation. Dunlop brought in more radical innovatory work in dance when Michael Clark and Company followed in the place, if not the manner, of the London Contemporary Dance Company. But if Clark angered dance enthusiasts on their first Festival appearance, they proved a splendid form of commemoration of the Glorious Revolution of 1688 in the subtly historically based *I am Curious, Orange* on their second visit. Even their most austere critics were somewhat mollified. 'Well, they danced', replied BBC Scotland's Neville Garden in answer to a query as to what happened in the show, adding kindly 'which was, as you might say, a step in the right direction.'

But the secret of Festival health is surely a policy of constructive and well-considered innovation, in place, in conception, or in theme. Tyrone Guthrie strikes this note in his *A Life in the Theatre* (1960) speaking of that first production of *The Thrie Estaites*:

One of the most pleasing effects of the performance was the physical relation of the audience to the stage. The audience did not look at the actors against a background of pictorial and illusionary scenery. Seated around three sides of the stage, they focussed upon the actors in the brightly lit acting area but the background was of the dimly lit rows of

people similarly focussed on the action. All the time, but unemphatically and by inference, each member of the audience was being ceaselessly reminded that he (sic) was not lost in an illusion, was not at the Court of King Humanitie in Sixteenth Century Scotland, but was, in fact, a member of a large audience, taking part, "assisting" as the French very properly express it, in a performance, a participant in a ritual.

To read Guthrie is to remind ourselves of how revolutionary in his day was so much that is taken for granted now. His thesis on the inappropriateness of illusion breaks down on a point a theatre director cannot know: that an audience's suspension of disbelief is necessarily intermittent, and a pageant-like production in the Assembly Hall now surrounds the consciousness of the audience, now permits its return to its own identity. The York Miracle Cycle at the Assembly Hall many years later captured this transience of identity: now one knew they were South Bank players, now one had a sense of being caught up in their world as medieval performers, now the Biblical themes asserted themselves to the exclusion of all else. Perhaps Guthrie was most signally refuted

when for Drummond's 'Vienna 1900' celebration Glasgow Citizens' Theatre staged in the Assembly Hall a lengthy, if brilliantly cut, version of Karl Kraus's *The Last Days of Mankind,* and the presence of Giles Havergal as Kraus, gaunt, despairing, sardonic and unfailingly courteous dominated the action throughout, giving the audience its identity as spectators in Vienna Café society: behind him the revelations of the progress of doom did their work but, while at times it became almost unbearably close to the bone, what came across was Kraus preaching to his deluded contemporaries, forever insistent on pointing lessons which he knew would forever be ignored. But whatever the limits of Guthrie's thesis, his sense of innovation was first-class and remains an inspiration for all the years that may follow him.

Sometimes, the innovatory possibilities of an idea have percolated into worlds of their own. Harewood produced literary events, though leaving the conception to chosen subordinates. Drummond followed suit, although much more the moving spirit of what happened, whoever might be charged with its immediate direction. Writers disputed

A little more than kin and less than kind - the meeting of two cousins who never met. Jill Bennett as Elizabeth I of England, John Fraser as Robert Dudley, Earl of Leicester, Leonard Maguire as Talbot, Earl of Shrewsbury, and Hannah Gordon in the title role of Frank Dunlop's production of MARY STUART (Schiller) in the Hall of the General Assembly of the Church of Scotland. 1987
ALEX 'TUG' WILSON

the meaning and magnitude of the word; TV moguls and critics wrangled over their rights and duties. From Drummond's revival of the old idea came the Edinburgh Book Festival which brings in every second year a huge succession of events and discussions, most appropriately commenced by Drummond himself in a fine exhibition of gloves-off dissection of a best-selling interviewee.

The Festival has its friends to whom it can never be sufficiently grateful. Cleo Laine is welcomed again and again for the strength, elasticity and sheer delight of her constantly changing repertoire but she won the Festival's heart in 1961 when, as Harewood recalls, she came in at two weeks' notice to replace Lotte Lenya who had flounced out of the Western Theatre Ballet/Scottish National Orchestra production of Kurt Weill's *Seven Deadly Sins* (' a favourite work of mine') in protest against Kenneth MacMillan's choreography. On the other hand, it was a long time before either the National Theatre of London or Tom Stoppard would be forgiven for declaring in print that its production of his adaptation of Nostroy as *On the Razzle* (with Penelope Keith as a most convincing boy apprentice) had premiered in London when it had, in fact, opened at the Edinburgh Festival. If the rest of the world is proud to acknowledge that its productions have premiered in Edinburgh when this is the case, Edinburgh is hardly likely to welcome London's sneaking pretence that a Festival booking amounts to a pre-opening provincial run. It was a sad fall in integrity for Stoppard, whose career had owed so much to Edinburgh; but the National Theatre's bad manners were simply a further reminder that nothing is to be expected from a pig but grunts. London must always be the place least likely to accord sympathy to Edinburgh, as sensitive Festival Directors should have remembered. They have spent too much time there, and they still aggrandise its parochialism by paying too much attention to it.

When all has been said, Edinburgh, for all of its crotchets, gentilities, Philistinism, sniffiness and parsimoniousness – and above all its complaceny – has made the Festival. The bulk of ticket-sales go to the residents of Edinburgh and the Lothians. Every Festival Director has cursed it frequently, and such reminiscences as those of Harewood and Guthrie abound with slightly patronising little sighs about the problems of dealing with the

natives. Edinburgh is still a victim of the effects of psychological colonialism among its immigrant cultural gurus as well as in the increasingly indignant hearts of its citizens. If Edinburgh is more complacent than Glasgow, it lacks Glasgow's self-confidence. Those who cared about it most, like Drummond, were hurt by it most. Hugh MacDiarmid, on occasion, switched his fire from the Festival's elitism to the Edinburgh audiences, who could always be relied on to turn out in their greatest numbers for the Tattoo.

The city fathers had a decidedly Victorian attitude to paternal authority and economy. The Drummond revolution ran up against the prevailing Tory preference for the few operas they knew and the musical compositions of which they had heard, and the embrace of the masses was hardly welcome in a philosophy that seemed to assess culture in

Sudden onslaught of Japanese hurricane in the early 17th century Mediterranean - the Ninagawa Company of Japan (successors to Toho) begin their TEMPEST in the Playhouse Theatre. 1988
ALEX 'TUG' WILSON

Sadie Aitken, Manager of the Gateway Theatre and, subsequently, at St Cecilia's Hall during its Festival presentations of reading and enactment in commemoration of great literary figures .
PAUL SHILLABEER

proportion to the numbers it excluded. When Scottish repudiation of Thatcherism hurled Labour into the seats of civic power Dunlop found the Edinburgh Labour Party still cherished the conviction that Festival was elitist, exclusive and egocentric. It took all of Dunlop's tact to convince his guardians that what they declared they sought was not only in existence but legitimately in existence. Meanwhile, Tattoo or no Tattoo, the Edinburgh public continued to make its way in increasing numbers to Festival and Fringe, Book Festival, Film Festival and Jazz Festival (it was sternly excluded from the Television Festival, where moguls and manipulators read papers to themselves). The Festival Director may still look enviously at Glasgow, where the civic worthies exude a far stronger aroma of immersion in their cultural products, and perhaps Frank Dunlop has quietly paid Glasgow his tribute by the importation of Glasgow comedy as well as of Glasgow comedians such as Rikki Fulton, magnificently collaborating across the centuries with Moliere. The fact remains that everyone has underestimated the loyalty of the Edinburgh public.

It is appropriate that Festival-lovers look back nostalgically to the moment of creation. But amid all the explanations of why Edinburgh was chosen – its good fortune in avoiding war damage, its former capital status unencumbered by bureaucratic mush-rooming, its distinguished, if somewhat, mausolear cultural emporia, its good fortune in having an enthusiast for the Festival idea in the Lord Provost when the first tentative steps were proposed – there also existed the often unspoken significance of Edinburgh tradition. Despite the best efforts of its Scotts and Stevensons, its Harvey Woods and Lord Camerons, Edinburgh is oddly unaware of some of the roots of its own identity and the world is, naturally, even less aware.

Did the Festival really begin in 1947? Bing believed it did, and so did Lord Provost Falconer, and so did Tyrone Guthrie, and the playwright James Bridie (whose fantasy in revolt against modernity, *Holy Isle*, was so successfully, if unpredictably, chosen by Frank Dunlop to commemorate the Bridie centenary in 1988). But, if this is the case, why did Mr Kennedy think he was singing at the Edinburgh Festival on August 9th, 1871 with songs to celebrate that year's centenarian, Sir Walter Scott? For what did the tone-deaf historian, Thomas Babington Macaulay, Member of Parliament for Edinburgh, take himself to have joined the enormous list of patrons, if not for what he was told was the Edinburgh Music Festival which opened on October 9th, 1843 in the New Music Hall at the Assembly Rooms on George Street? And why did Sir Walter Scott add his name to the list of patrons on October 26th, 1824 if he did not believe the claim that they were giving their blessing to the Edinburgh Music Festival?

And when, as Lord Keynes put it, in the long run we are all dead, Edinburgh will remain. And so should its Festival, if it deepens its slowly growing awareness that it exists because of, not in spite of, Edinburgh.

Owen Dudley Edwards
University of Edinburgh
Lent, 1990

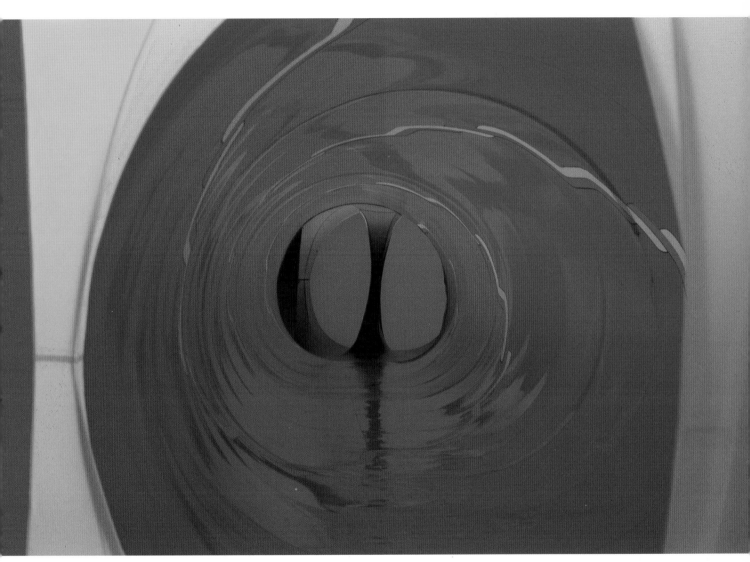

Manadarah's Theatre of Pneumatic Art
created a maze-like effect of multi-coloured
plastic tunnels in the Meadows. Fringe

Left: St Louis Opera Theatre brought an opportunity to see (and hear), for the first time, the work of Stephen Paulus, one of America's most promising young composers. THE POSTMAN ALWAYS RINGS TWICE, his first full length opera, with libretto by Colin Graham, is based on the novel by James M. Cain. King's Theatre

Right: Dance according to the Japanese Buto School gave distinctive style to the performances of Muteki Sha in their production of NIWA (The Garden) at the Assembly Rooms. Fringe

Below: Ready Wrapped at the YWCA. Duncan Whiteman's READY WRAPPED SCULPTURE SHOW created some interesting images. Fringe

Right: A dramatic moment from The Hungarian State Ballet's presentation of Anton Fodor's PROBA - with music by Bach and Gabor Presser - based on Nikos Kazantzakis's novel 'Christ Recrucified'.

Below: The exhibition, at The National Museum of Antiquities ,VIENNA 1900, was shown in tandem with a series of lectures and seminars on the theme of Vienna at the turn of the century.

Next page: The castle as a mere detail - The Glenlivet Fireworks Concert in Princes Street Gardens, 1983.

Michael Clark in an early Fringe
performance before he became 'official' on
the Festival programme.

Right: The Three Vices, Flatterie, Deceit and
Falsehood (Walter Carr, John Grieve and
Gregor Fisher) in Sir David Lyndsay's ANE
SATYRE OF THE THRIE ESTAITES, directed by
Tom Fleming at the Hall of the General
Assembly of the Church of Scotland.

Below: David Warrilow in A PIECE OF
MONOLOGUE at the Church Hill Theatre, as
part of the Samuel Beckett Season presented
by the Harold Klurman Theatre of New York.

Above: Rudolf Nureyev danced in, and also directed, HARLEQUIN, MAGICIAN OF LOVE at the Playhouse Theatre, in the Paris Opera Ballet's triple bill COMMEDIA DELL'ARTE, THREE BALLETS ON A THEME.

Left: Ekkehard Schall as Bertolt Brecht's GALILEO GALILEI for the Berliner Ensemble at the King's Theatre.

Right: Eli Wallach made a Festival appearance in 1984 in Murray Schisgal's play, TWICE AROUND THE PARK, directed by Arthur Storch at the King's Theatre.

Below: Beverly Evans as Madame Flora in the Washington Opera production of Gian Carlo Menotti's THE MEDIUM at the King's Theatre.

Far right: Eva Ciharova as Titania entertains Ales Kondelka as Bottom in the Midsummer Night's Dream sequence from The Black Light Theatre of Prague's A WEEK OF DREAMS at the Royal Lyceum Theatre.

Above: The heart warming Children's Music Theatre recreated THE TOWER OF BABEL at St Mary's Cathedral in one of their many Festival and Fringe spectacular conquests.

Right: Lord Rama and his wife, Sita, as performed by Phadej Plubgrasonk and Sonying Vechsuruck of the Royal Thai Classical Dancers in their performance of THE KHON DRAMA at the King's Theatre.

Above: Neeme Jarvi rehearsing, at the Usher Hall, for his début as the Scottish National Orchestra's Musical Director and Principal Conductor .

Right: Anne Howells (Diana) and Linda Ormiston (Aurora) in Scottish Opera's production of Cavalli's ORION at the King's Theatre, directed by Peter Wood.

Dieter Hulse (Siegfried) and Jutta Deutschland (Odette) in Tom Schilling's revolutionary production of SWAN LAKE with the Komische Oper Ballet from Berlin, at the Playhouse Theatre.

The grasses changing colour in response to the 1984 Glenlivet Fireworks Concert, Princes Street Gardens.

Right: Chabrier's opera-bouffe, L'ETOILE, with words by E. Leterrier and A.Vanloo, was performed at the King's Theatre by the Opéra de Lyon.

Below: Mikijiro Hira as the Toho Company's MACBETH, directed by the great Yukio Ninagawa, at the Royal Lyceum Theatre.

Far left: Rikki Fulton, Anne Kidd and Paul Young provide A WEE TOUCH OF CLASS in the Perth Theatre Company's production in the Church Hill Theatre. The adaptation into Scots of Moliere's 'Le Bourgeois Gentilhomme' was effected by 'Rabaith' (otherwise known as Rikki Fulton and Denise Coffey).

Left: Scottish sculptor, George Wyllie, samples A DAY DOWN A GOLDMINE at the Assembly Rooms, George Street. Fringe

Below: Beverly Evans in Connecticut Grand Opera's production of Gian Carlo Menotti's THE CONSUL at Leith Theatre.

Right: SYMBOLS OF POWER AT THE TIME OF STONEHENGE. The late, great Bill Gibb's costume design for the exhibition in the National Museum of Antiquities of Scotland.

Above: Veritie and Chastitie in the Hall of the General Assembly of the Church of Scotland. Anne Kristen and Edith MacArthur as the Two Virtues in the Edinburgh International Festival production of Sir John Lyndsay's ANE SATYRE OF THE THRIE ESTAITES.

Right: Alec Heggie leads as THE WALLACE, an EIF production, in collaboration with The Scottish Theatre Company, of Sydney Goodsir Smith's play at the Hall of the General Assembly.

Timothy Furst, Paul David Magid, Howard Jay Patterson, Sam Williams and Randy Nelson as THE FLYING BROTHERS KARAMAZOV at the Royal Lyceum Theatre.

John Gordon Sinclair in the Theatre of Comedy production of WOMEN ALL OVER, John Wells's English version of Feydeau's farce, LE DINDON. King's Theatre

Right: Find the missing links. Colourscape's translucent plastic tunnels filled the bowling green by the National Gallery of Scotland with unusual colour. Fringe

Below: SLAUGHTER ON McDOUGAL STREET. The Groupe de Recherche Chorégraphique of the Paris Opéra Ballet experiment, at the Playhouse Theatre, with something completely different from their many classical programmes.

Above: Peter Darrell's new production of CARMEN for Scottish Ballet received its world premiere at the Playhouse Theatre with Christine Camillo expressing emotional freedom in the lead role.

Right: Glenlivet Fireworks painting the town red.

Top left: The folk group Rumillajta played MUSIC OF THE ANDES at the Assembly Rooms. Fringe

Below left: The Scottish entertainer and impressario, Jimmy Logan, made his Festival debut as another famous Scottish entertainer, Sir Harry Lauder, at the Portobello Town Hall.

Below right: The legendary Scottish cartoon character, 'Oor Wullie', presumably in the title role in THE ENTERPRISING SCOT exhibition at the Royal Scottish Academy, thus proving culture breaks all barriers.

Right: Bellany et bel - ami. John Bellany, at home in Edinburgh, beside his own portrait of Festival Director, Frank Dunlop.

Above: World theatre from Spain came to the Royal Lyceum Theatre in 1985 in the form of the Nuria Espert Company. The great Spanish actress and director played the title role, and directed her own company, in Lorca's tragedy of YERMA from his 'Trilogy of the Spanish Earth'.

Right: The Toho Company returned, triumphant, to the 1986 Festival with Yukio Ninagawa's interpretation of MEDEA, in the Courtyard of the Old College of the University of Edinburgh. Mikijiro Hira, who played Macbeth in 1985, is Medea.

Left: Ariel crowns the National Gallery. Vera Simon's pneumatic art sculpture ARIEL CROWN gives a new look to the National Gallery of Scotland thus rekindling respect for its previous condition.

Far left: Lyon Opéra Ballet's CINDERELLA, choreographed by Maguy Marin, one of the most innovative choreographers in France today was, arguably, the most unusual and inventive production of that ballet seen for a long time with the dancers skilfully disguised with masks to look like children. Playhouse Theatre

Left: Ewa Glowacka, Prima Ballerina of the Ballet of the Great Theatre, Warsaw, as Princess Aurora in SLEEPING BEAUTY at the Playhouse Theatre.

Below:Trinidad Sevillano and Virginie Alberti as two old swans in DROP YOUR PEARLS AND HOG IT,GIRL, a light-hearted look at ballet's obsession with birds, which Michael Clark choreographed for London Festival Ballet's LFB2 at the Royal Lyceum Theatre.

The Stary Theatre, Krakow, juxtapose CRIME AND PUNISHMENT at St Bride's Centre.

Anne-Marie Mühle as Amneris, and Margareta Edstrom as Aida in the Folk Opera of Stockholm's production of Verdi's AIDA at Leith Theatre.

The Oxford Playhouse Theatre Company's
HAMLET with David Threlfall in the title role
and Jean March as Gertrude. The Hall of the
General Assembly.

Left: Sergei Slonimsky provided music and Yakov Gordin words for the Russian-language 'ballad opera' version of the story of MARIA STUART performed at the King's Theatre by the Maly Theatre of Leningrad.

Right: Yukio Ninagawa, of Toho Macbeth fame, appealing to the spirit of Euripides for good weather for his open-air production of MEDEA.

Joan Knight's revival of John Home's DOUGLAS with James Telfer as Douglas in the incomparable setting of the Signet Library, Parliament Square. This came after an interval of almost 230 years, although there had been one previous production in 1950 with Sybil Thorndike and Lewis Casson.

BODAS DE SANGE (BLOOD WEDDING) at the Royal Lyceum Theatre. Jose Luis Gomez's production of Lorca's masterpiece broke language barriers in another powerful offering in the World Theatre Season at the Festival of 1986.

Fireworks 1986 style - or else select the play of your choice to be symbolised thus.

Right: Jorma Hynninen as the cursed, hunchback jester in Verdi's RIGOLETTO with the Finnish National Opera at the King's Theatre.

Far right: Viktoria Mullova, the young Russian violinist, contemplates her second Festival performance in 1986. She played the Brahms Violin Concerto in D major, Op 77, with the Swedish Radio Orchestra at the Usher Hall.

Below: The Gorky Theatre of Leningrad's great actor Evgeny Lebedev as Kholstomer in their production of THE HISTORY OF A HORSE at the King's Theatre.

Left: Donal McCann as Captain Jack Boyle
and John Kavanagh as Joxer Daly in the
Dublin Gate Theatre's production of Sean
O'Casey's JUNO AND THE PAYCOCK at the
Royal Lyceum Theatre. As the playwright's
widow, Eileen, said after the – almost
definitive – performance, 'Sean would have
been so pleased.'

Above: In 1987, the quatercentenary of the
death of Mary Queen of Scots, the Edinburgh
Festival presented, in association with the
Scottish Theatre Company, the Festival
Director's production of Schiller's MARY
STUART. Here, Sir Edward Mortimer
(Jonathon Morris), nephew of her gaoler, Sir
Amias Paulet, Governor of Fotheringay,
declares to Mary (Hannah Gordon) that he
is not the enemy but a friend.

Far left: Rudolf Nureyev as Petrouchka with the Ballet Théâtre Français de Nancy at the Playhouse Theatre.

Above left: Lena Willman, a magnificent Queen of the Night, in the Folkopera of Stockholm production of Mozart's THE MAGIC FLUTE at Leith Theatre.

Left: Rudolf Nureyev and Alexandra Wells interpret Nijinsky's choregrahy to Debussy's music in L'APRES - MIDI D'UN FAUNE when the Ballet Théâtre Français de Nancy presented a programme of HOMAGE TO LES BALLETS RUSSES AND DIAGHILEV at the Playhouse Theatre.

Above: John Ogden concentrates on Rachmaninov's Piano Concerto No 2 in C minor, Op 18 which he played at the Usher Hall with the BBC Scottish Symphony Orchestra, conducted by Jerzy Maksymiuk.

Top left: Séance Friction at the Assembly Rooms in George Street. Fringe

Below far left: The Face on the Festival Floor – or Pavement –while the rain keeps off.

Below left: The largest prop on the Fringe was the claim of Théâtre de la Basoche when they brought the bath with them from France for their award-winning LE LAVOIR, most appropriately staged at the Abbeymount Washhouse.

Above: Hideki Noda wrote, directed and starred in the Yume no yuminsha Company's DESCENT OF THE BRUTES. A bizarre story about a boxer called Apollo Juichi (Brute the First). It infuriated some critics and delighted others.

Far left: Ji Zhenghua was an impressive MACBETH, Shanghai style, when the Shanghai Kunju Theatre came to the Leith Theatre with their version of the Scottish Play.

Left: Shanghai Kunju Theatre, PEONY PAVILION, transforming Leith Theatre.

Above: The stuff that dreams are made of – Nutcracker National Ballet of Finland at the King's Theatre.

Above: Stomu Yamash'ta, the renowned percussionist from Japan, in a resounding moment during one of his performances at St Bride's Centre.

Right: Glenlivet fireworks, 1987 – a cocktail not to be taken before driving.

Left: LA MORTE DI RUGGIERO DELL'AQUILA BIANCA, or The Death of Sir Ruggiero of the White Eagle, as realised by the puppets of the Compagnia dei Pupi Siciliani di Nino

Cutticchio – a family affair with Nino, Rosa, and Tiziana Cuttichio, at the Church Hill Theatre.

Above: Mauro Bigonzetti as the Chinese Conjurer in Aterballetto's production of PARADE, a remarkable combination of three great talents, Jean Cocteau (story), Leonide Massine (choreography), and Eric Satie (music), at the King's Theatre.

Left: The National (formerly Children's) Youth Music Theatre in their production of THE LITTLE RATS, an exciting and stimulating musical play, performed at George Square Theatre, under the dedicated direction of Jeremy James Taylor.

Above: The Matsuyama Ballet's appearance at the Playhouse Theatre provided a rare chance to see the prima ballerina Yoko Morishita in the title role of GISELLE for which she had won the Laurence Olivier prize in 1985.

Jean-Marie Frin in P'TIT ALBERT presented by the Comédie de Caen at Drummond Community High School. Fringe

John Duykers as Mao Tse-Tung, entering through his own mouth, in the Houston Grand Opera's production of NIXON IN CHINA at the Playhouse Theatre.

*Above: The Brunton Theatre Company
brought HOLY ISLE to the Church Hill Theatre
as part of the James Bridie Centenary
celebrations, directed imaginatively by
Charles Nowosielski.*

Far left: DANIEL AND THE LIONS, not yet in their den, but in Greyfriars Kirk when the Ensemble for Early Music performed there under Paul Hildebrand and Bobby Small.

Left: The Ninagawa Company brought a spectacular Japanese TEMPEST to the Playhouse Theatre. The boat is about to break up amid thunder and lightning in a tempestuous sea.

Below left: AS THE PIANO PLAYS from the Tmu-na Theatre, Israel, ran at the Assembly Rooms, George Street. Fringe

Below: DEAD MARILYN. Peter Stack in drag for the title role in Deadline Promotions' production about Marilyn Monroe at Calton Studios. Fringe

Right: Glenlivet Fireworks 1988, Princes Street Gardens.

Left: Simon Rattle dressed for rehearsal to conduct The City of Birmingham Symphony Orchestra (the resident orchestra of the 1989 Festival) at the Usher Hall.

Below: Olwen Fouere as Salomé in the Dublin Gate Theatre's stylised production of Oscar Wilde's play, directed by Steven Berkoff, and presented at the Royal Lyceum Theatre, unfortunately in English instead of the original French.

Far left: DIMONIS in George Heriot's. Spectacular devils of a more unusual nature than the common schoolboy version were much in evidence when Els Comediants provided two evenings of spectacle in the grounds of George Heriot's School with music, fireworks, and very acrobatic performers.

Left: Nikolai Gubenko in the title role of the Moscow Taganka Theatre's production of Alexander Pushkin's, BORIS GODUNOV, directed by Yuri Lyubimov at Leith Theatre.

Below left: Archaos, a new circus group to appear in Festival 1990 – here seen on the Fringe, 1989.

Left: Jutland Opera's production of THE DIVINE CIRCUS combines the work of many international talents with music by Per Norgard and words by Ted Hughes, William Shakespeare and Frederich Nietsche. Leith Theatre.

Above: Janie Parker, a gracefully classical Odette, in the Houston's Ballet's SWAN LAKE at the Playhouse Theatre.

Above: Johann Kresnik, the innovative and highly imaginative theatre director who believes in 'Choreographic Theatre', or the development of moving images on stage, brought the Bremer Theatre to the King's with his production of MACBETH. The gigantic tables, chairs and teapots, under, over, and around which the mobile cast moved, left audiences shocked but not silenced.

Right: C'EST DIMANCHE , it must be the Compagnie Jerome Deschamps at the King's Theatre. Written and directed by Jerome Deschamps with Jean-Marc Bihour and Christine Pignet.

Left: Francisco Bobollo, delights the audience with a touch of Spanish guitar in LA CHULAPONA, a high-spirited,dramatic comedy with an authentic flavour of 19th century Madrid, presented by the National Opera of Spain, Teatro La Zarzuela, Madrid

Far left: Ravi Shankar, the celebrated Indian musician, appeared at the Usher Hall for a 50th anniversary concert.

Far left: THE GARDEN OF EARTHLY DELIGHTS was performed by the Music Theatre Group, directed by Martha Clarke, at the Royal Lyceum before ecstatic audiences.

Left: Amparo Rivelles in the title role of LA CELESTINA by Fernando de Rojas in the Compania Nacional Teatro Clasico's production at the Royal Lyceum Theatre.

Left: The versatile Jose Antonio, artistic director and principal dancer of the Ballet Nacional de Espana, performs with typical exhuberance in a programme of Spanish dance and music, which included the famous BOLERO, and ALBORADA DEL GRACIOSO, a ballet specially commissioned for Jose Antonio, and also featuring the music of Ravel.

Below: Stary Theatre, Krakow, made a welcome return to the 1989 Festival with THE DYBUK, based on the play by Solomon Ansky, the 19th century Jewish writer who concerned himself with the legends and stories of Jews living in the countryside. Here Krzysztof Globisz plays the part of Chanan, a scholar in Brinica who is searching for the path to Truth.

Right: Political Ecumenism – Fireworks, 1989